SAY THIS,
NOT THAT

SAY THIS, NOT THAT

HOW TO BUILD TRUST AND MOTIVATE OTHERS WITH THE RIGHT CHOICE OF WORDS

DAVE DURAND

A Crossroad Book
The Crossroad Publishing Company
New York

The Crossroad Publishing Company
www.CrossroadPublishing.com

In continuation of our 200-year tradition of independent publishing, The Crossroad Publishing Company proudly offers a variety of books with strong, original voices and diverse perspectives. The viewpoints expressed in our books are not necessarily those of The Crossroad Publishing Company, any of its imprints or of its employees. No claims are made or responsibility assumed for any health or other benefit.

Printed in the United States of America.
The text of this book is set in Web Fusion
The display face is Sabon

Project Management by
The Crossroad Publishing Company
John Jones
For this edition numerous people have shared their talents and ideas, and we gratefully acknowledge Dave Durand, who has been most gracious during the course of our cooperation.

We thank especially:
Cover design: George Foster   Text design: Web Fusion
Copyediting: Sylke Jackson   Printing: Versa Press

Message development, text development, package, and market positioning by The Crossroad Publishing Company

Cataloging-in-Publication Data is available from the Library of Congress

Books published by The Crossroad Publishing Company may be purchased at special quantity discount rates for classes and institutional use. For information, please e-mail info@CrossroadPublishing.com
ISBN 13: 978-0-8245-2625-2

14 13 12 11

CONTENTS

Part One: Getting Started

Part Two: Say This, Not That...

Part Three: Motivating Others to Be Their Best

Part One
GETTING STARTED

INTRODUCTION

WHEN IT COMES to communication, good intentions are not enough.

I recently sat in the back of a packed hotel conference room, watching a newly promoted 30-something man attempting to energize and motivate his organization. He had attracted a well-qualified team of up and comers, all of whom would be considered the type of talent you should work hard to retain. He himself was very skilled. By the age of thirty he had built a multimillion dollar business. His audience liked and admired him. As he stood at the podium, he intended to empower his young team of leaders by inspiring them to pursue an aggressive career track. He wanted to share with them how much they would enjoy being in his shoes, how it would make all the hard work worthwhile. Gesturing with his outstretched hand to indicate everyone in the entire room, he said, "You would not believe how great it feels to have the power over all of you like I do. You would love it."

Good intentions, wrong words, lousy results.

Because I was outside of his organization, and I knew the point he was trying to communicate, I found it easy to separate the deeper meaning from his poorly chosen words. Unfortunately, many people in his organization could not see past the words. They didn't hear that he was trying to give them something for their own benefit.

All they heard was an egotist gloating over his power. Of course, there was no mass exodus, no racing for the exits. The result was a more subtle doubt that moved through the audience and undermined his message—that day and in his later interactions. That's the way it usually goes. The wrong words we use fester, bubble up, and eventually spill out all over the good intentions we had to begin with. Others doubt us, and we ourselves feel unfairly judged.

Addition by subtraction is a truism when it comes to motivation. After two decades of studying human interactions in organizational settings, I have determined that most of us would double our productivity if we just said 50% fewer stupid things. But the absence of stupid remarks only gets us so far. To produce the results we want, there are times when we need to nail the words on the head in order to get our point across. Avoidance isn't enough. It's not enough *not to say that*. We need a set of instruments for communicating effectively—we need to *say this*.

Listening to these instruments being used well is like listening to the finest of symphonies.

As part of my work with struggling companies, I once listened to a CEO frame his vision for entering what everyone knew was going to be a turbulent time for his company, following a time of great prosperity. Addressing the uncertainty head-on, he said the following to his team of five senior managers:

"Over the past two years, we have had the perfect confluence of events for our company to prosper. You led well. Our results were impressive, and you are to be commended. I recognize that the economic climate during those years was so good that, whether here or at other companies, many other less senior executives may have been able to produce what we did in our respective roles. I include myself in that. I compliment them without any negative reflection on our own work, but with the intention of contrasting the difference between those days and the days ahead. While several others might have been able to do what we did in the past, only five can do the tasks we have ahead of us, and those five are you: precisely you. Your experience and skills were well suited to the high times, but my confidence in your ability to navigate the coming storm is what allows me to sleep well at night. This is where your greatness will truly shine."

The executives felt appreciated, challenged, and ready to take responsibility to face the coming days—all from a speech that lasted less than 90 seconds. It set the stage for increased trust despite longer hours and increased stress.

What makes the difference between the wrong words and the right ones? It isn't always the words themselves. As you've probably figured out in your own work, the concept of perfect words is a myth. With the exception of Please and Thank You, there are no magic words. Some of us have discovered the hard way that the same words that make one person feel inspired, safe, and confident might bring out exactly the opposite emotions in another person. Words that work between an employee and a manager would be likely to get someone thrown out of the house if they were said between husband and wife. In some ways, words really are like art, and not everyone will respond in the same way.

But there is also a science to words, and it's this science that gives me the confidence to tell you to *Say This, Not That*. I will write from the perspective of leadership in organizational settings. This is my long-standing area of study and experience. My experience extends beyond formal leadership and includes training and coaching settings. These settings add a particularly important and universally applicable perspective, which I will explain more fully in the coming chapters. And in these settings, I've noticed that some words simply don't work, no matter how much you want them to, and other words do. If you want to be effective as a leader, you have to learn to tell the difference.

For 20 years I have also been a family man and the father of six kids. In some ways, the language we use in business is different than the language we use at home. But there are still important points of similarity. I have found that by using business relationships as a model on one end of the spectrum, and family relationships as a model on the other, it's possible to cover most of the territory in between. So with a bit of adaptability, you too will be able to translate these scenarios, which I draw primarily from business, into the rest of your life quite well. I know these words will work for you—they've worked for me, and I've seen them work for countless people I've coached, in business settings, in churches and synagogues, and at home.

In this book, I'm assuming that your intentions are good, you want the people around you to succeed, and you're trying to find the best way to make that happen. You can Google "worst things to say" and get hundreds of suggestions about the cruel things people say to each other in various settings, whether it's romance or business. If you're cruel, the list of things you might say, but shouldn't, could fill a library. As I mentioned, good intentions are not enough, but they are a necessary beginning. This book will not help a negative person become a good one. I believe that it will help a good person learn how to communicate well, so that all good intentions can be put into action.

The power of words is enormous. Great quotes and inspirational speeches have had the power to change the course of nations and rally people from bondage to independence. On the other hand, foolish quotes have also echoed through time. Common threads run through the great quotes; the foolish ones have some similarities with each other as well. In this book, we'll investigate the difference, why we *Say This* but *Not That*. Our goal is that, when we're done, you'll speak like the CEO above, able to inspire and motivate even in the toughest of situations. Let's dive right in with a few simple key basics to get you on your way.

THINGS YOU CAN SAY – RIGHT AWAY!

To get you started, here are eight surprising examples of *Say This, Not That*. I recommend reading the entire book, but if you're curious, I give you the page number so you can learn more right away about why each one works (or fails).

Say This:
"I trust you to do this."
Not That:
"You can trust me."
(p. 74)

Say This:
"However..."
Not That:
"But..."
(p. 45)

Say This:
"I am going to deliver on this."
Not That:
"You have my word."
(p. 78)

Say This:
"I shouldn't have said that."
Not That:
"Forget you heard that."
(p. 88)

Say This:
"I'm sorry."
Not That:
"I'm sorry that you feel that way."
(p. 81)

Say This:
"I'm really impressed by this."
Not That:
"You're really good at this."
(p. 95)

Say This:
"Tell me more about that."
Not That:
"Wow, neat."
(p. 57)

Say This:
"I need to discuss this with you to get us back on track."
Not That:
"Don't take this personally."
(p. 36)

∻ One ∻

MAKE THE CONNECTION

ALL OF US STRUGGLE to find the right words. One mother talks to another about how she tried to discipline her teenager after she found her drinking. "Did I say the right thing?" A principal talks with a close friend about having to let an employee go. "How do I find the words?" It's natural for us to turn to others for advice—as long as it's confidential—and even more natural for us to want to ask our mentors, teachers, and coaches for the words that work. After all, we trust them. To get where they are, they must have done something right.

At the same time, it's never just about the words. It's about the connection you make. If you fail to make a connection, the best words in the world won't matter. And if you do make a connection, even a blundering error will be forgiven.

I'll never forget watching a stump speech Ronald Reagan gave as he campaigned for his second term as president. He was tired and had been traveling too much, and he needed a break, but the campaign was not over yet, so he trudged forward to give his well-oiled stump speech. During one stop, just as he began, a heckler started yelling out. This was not just a typical heckler who wanted to exercise a little freedom of speech and make a point—he was trying to shout the President down so he couldn't even give his message. President Reagan initially ignored the heckler; then, realizing the guy was not going to relent, he yelled out the less than articulate statement, "Aauugghh, Shhhut up!"

Those words, said in exactly that way, would have without question knocked most candidates completely out of any campaign. But after Reagan yelled out his rebuke, the crowd erupted with enthusiasm. He intuitively understood that the rest of the crowd was as irritated by the heckler as he was, so his rebuke helped his audience connect with him on a visceral level.

The importance of a connection with your subject is crucial. I would go as far as to say that without it, 95% of what you say is wasted. Researchers are discovering this more and more, in particular as the Internet allows for unprecedented levels of information to be exchanged without necessarily increasing communication and understanding. As Bonnie A. Nardi at UC Irvine has shown in her investigation of the ways that people connect personally via technology, connection matters.[1] What's true for electronic media is even more true for live interaction—without a connection, information does not flow.

So how do you make a connection? Through feelings of affinity, commitment, and attention. Let's break down these words so we can gather the fullest insight and develop the skills it takes to build a connection.

TIP 1: Before you begin a personal interaction, give some thought to what you can do to play down anything that communicates "I can't relate," while highlighting things that say "I can relate".

Affinity:

1. Feeling of identification: a natural liking for or identification with somebody or something
2. Connection: a similarity or connection between people or things

Affinity is another way of saying: similarity, resemblance, likeness, empathy, sympathy, fellow feeling, attraction, and kinship. The point is clear. Your relationship to the person who is listening to you must be tethered at least a little, or you'll lose the desired outcome. The stronger the connection is, the greater the margin of error for wrong word choices.

Companies that excel in customer service understand this well. In one case, a company that specialized in wedding gifts had done several internal audits on its customer service record. Each time the company rated at the highest level, an A+. The rating was based on whether or not the complaint was rectified. For example, if a product was delivered to the wrong address, the company tracked it down and made sure it arrived at the appropriate address. Then the customer was surveyed to ask if her complaint had been satisfactorily addressed. The answers the company's surveyors got back supported the A+ grade, but they noticed something odd. Why, if the company was getting all these satisfactory reviews from upset customers, was return business so low from them? The leaders set out to find the answer, bringing in an outside consultant to review customer service practices.

The outside firm quickly identified one primary area where a small change could create an enormous difference. Up to that point, the customer service reps had been trained to speak calmly and to encourage angry or upset customers to calm down. They were not the first company to do this – many companies used to encourage this approach to dealing with dissatisfied buyers. This practice was replaced with the new one. A rep would let the customer vent while the rep jumped on the bandwagon and got upset *alongside the customer.* In other words, in the past a conversation might have gone like this:

Customer (yelling): "I'm so angry with your stupid company for delivering my gift to the wrong address. It messed up my entire plan!"

Rep: "Okay, please calm down and I'll see what I can do for you."

That approach destroyed whatever connection there might have been, or prevented it from forming. The new rep approach sounded more like this:

Customer (yelling): "I'm so angry with your stupid company for delivering my gift to the wrong address. It ruined my entire plan!"

Rep: "What, it was late?"

Customer: "Yes, it was late, and now I'm spending hours to fix the mess!"

Rep: "That's awful. I can't believe that. I'd be so angry if I were you. I'm sure that ruined your entire plan. I tell you what. I'm going to get to the bottom of this here and make sure whoever was responsible knows how inconvenient it was for you. I know it's of little consolation, but I'll make sure you get you product tomorrow."

Think about that approach. It has a "wow, she really gets me!" feel to it that builds a connection rapidly. The first approach motivates the customer to make her point more clearly and with greater conviction so that she can feel understood – she knows that she isn't getting her point across. Being misunderstood usually results in a bigger gap between both parties. *Being understood* is the pinnacle of being connected.

So, what are the words that connect us? Anything that says: I can feel (or at least understand) your, pain, joy, frustration, irritation, or any other emotion.

Say This

1. I understand.

2. I get what you are saying.

3. That makes sense.

4. I can see where you are coming from.

5. I bet that's frustrating. / How great, I am sure you are so happy.

Another way to say this same thing is in the wording of marriage counselors. You've probably seen this idea on TV. Therapists coach spouses to "validate" each other when communicating. Many people struggle with that concept because they confuse validating (and, for that matter, most of the phrases on the list above) with *agreeing with* the other party. And many people don't want to lie ("I don't agree with them!"), so they refuse to validate. This shows good intentions but misses the point. None of these statements require agreeing about *anything*. Even example 3, "that makes sense," is not necessarily a confirmation of agreement. It shows that you can understand the outline of what someone is trying to say, but it doesn't mean you are giving the person the last word.

This can be a difficult concept for people who overanalyze in their heads. They might simply say, "But I *don't agree*. Are you telling me to agree with something that is factually wrong?" No, of course not. Look at it this way. When I was 4 years old, I heard my dad ask my mom to pass the salt after she commented that her dinner was very hot. I made the immediate association that salt was used to cool food down. The conclusion was supported by hearing others at the table say they didn't like pepper because it was too hot! Obviously, eventually I figured out that salt and pepper had nothing to do with temperature. But given my experiences with salt, it made sense to draw the conclusions I did, despite the fact that I was entirely wrong. This is just as true for the intelligent grown-ups you work with every day. Much of what they believe does make sense, even if it's wrong. You don't have to agree with wrong concepts. If you want to make the connection, you only have to see it from their perspective. So validation is about understanding where the other party is coming from, not agreeing with her outcome.

Tip 2: When in doubt, play it safe by being short on words and long on smiles. Establishing a feeling of commitment is more often about avoiding the *Not That* part of *Say This, Not That*. This takes the pressure off because we are all intuitively hardwired more to identify the wrong words and actions than to sense when the right words are missing.

Commitment

1. Responsibility: something that takes up time or energy, especially an obligation

2. Loyalty: devotion or dedication, e.g. to a cause, person, or relationship

The synonyms for commitment are: promise, pledge, obligation, assurance, and dedication. These words may sound like heavy lifting—especially for men, in light of the old axiom that men are afraid of commitment. In reality, though, both men and women fear commitment, because being committed means being obligated. The idea of being obligated to everyone we interact with is daunting. So here's the key to unlocking that fear on an emotional level. The true commitment you must make is to only one person—and that person is you. If you make a commitment to yourself to interact with everyone in your path in a respectful, dignified way that shows interest in them, you'll build a habit and way about you that is intoxicating.

This commitment radiates as confidence and conviction. Presenting yourself with a lack of confidence or conviction can make you appear noncommittal—even when you are committed. Whenever we feel one way but are accused of intentions which are the opposite, we experience emotional distress and can become defensive, making the scenario even worse.

In one particular organization I worked with, two people had just completed their initial sales training seminar. The first, Kelly, was a young, inexperienced woman fresh out of college. With the exception of what she learned in training, she knew virtually nothing about sales. The second was Eric, a weathered middle-aged man who had two decades of successful selling experience under his belt. Nathan, the sales trainer, was a younger man in his late twenties. He was in his role primarily because of his enthusiasm and charisma, not due to past sales accomplishments.

Throughout the seminar, Eric asked Nathan many questions along the lines of: "What did you do when you ran into a customer who…?" Nathan began to feel that Eric, who had years of experience, was challenging his abilities. Sensing the competitive nature of the questions Nathan became insecure. He reacted by dodging the questions and saying things like, "Well, the best thing to do is to…" Eric recognized the pattern and felt disconnected from Nathan. He felt that Nathan was different from him and expressed it by saying, "Nathan talks a good game but I have been in the field. He doesn't really know what he is saying." Eric failed within the first two months and moved on.

Kelly, on the other hand, never picked up on Nathan's lack of experience, and she observed everything he said in training. She commented on Nathan, "I love his enthusiasm. He's so smart. I want to do everything he says because if I do, I know I'll be successful." She was correct. She skyrocketed as the top rep and never looked back.

This is a case we can learn a lot from. The same sales trainer, teaching the same information, connected to one rep and she succeeded. He failed to connect to the other, and that rep failed. The connection we make with others has a profound effect. Through experience Nathan later learned to adapt his communication skills to make stronger connections with more experienced trainees. He began stating with confidence that his expertise was not in the field but as a trainer, so that he could translate the experiences of the top sales people in the company and present them in a usable fashion for new recruits. His confident approach was a commitment he made to himself, but it was also raised his level of connection with experienced recruits. The appropriate success followed.

Attention:

1. Concentration; mental focus, serious consideration, or concentration

2. Notice or interest

3. Appropriate treatment: care, tending

Synonyms: notice, consideration, thought, awareness, thought, mind, consideration

Mike was a popular CEO who had a plethora of great practices for building a connection to his team. Among those practices was sending birthday cards and calling more than 400 people each year on their birthdays to wish them well. On one hand, it was a call that included zero content regarding the business. What a perfect "not that" scenario! On the other hand, the call was all personal, which is a perfect *Say This* scenario.

Compare this with a common practice of an unpopular yet absolutely brilliant CEO, Tim. He had a terrible habit of reading his e-mail while he talked to his team. He did this both over the phone and in face-to-face conversations. It was clear that he wasn't very interested in what his team members had to say. He didn't give them the attention and thoughtfulness they deserved. In getting to know Tim, I discovered that he did this because he was so intellectually advanced, he genuinely could concentrate on various issues simultaneously. For example, when I pressed him about conversations he'd had, I was amazed to hear how clearly he remembered the details. He definitely was not "not paying attention." But that didn't matter. The people he engaged with felt unappreciated and therefore disconnected, and all the focus in the world could not change that.

I've seen this same pattern elsewhere. I've coached individuals who need very little time to process the input, thoughts, and ideas of others. Sometimes they have the ability to process ideas so quickly that they barely need to hear the completion of a thought in order to accurately access situations. So they immediately provide feedback and answers—sound answers.

However, their rapid responses are met with animosity—they seem insincere. You should avoid falling into this trap yourself. Make sure your subjects *feel* a connection by communicating to them that you are paying attention. You may need to practice pausing, restating the idea, and validating it before moving forward. This sacrifices nothing of the content of your reply, but it does help you make the necessary connection so you can build trust.

Show your subject that they have your undivided attention. An executive I worked with named Bruce is a great example of this. He is known for making everyone he talks to feel like they are the most important person in the room – or for that matter, in the congregation. I once asked him how he was so sincere in his approach. I commented on his exceptional eye contact, head tilt, and responses, which conveyed a total interest in the other person. Under my breath I mentioned that it was a gift. He replied very clearly that it was not a gift – it was a skill that he'd developed carefully over 30 years. He went on to say that he learned this skill from his mentor, who did the same thing.

The fact that he learned the practice as a skill did not in any way diminish his sincerity. In fact, his efforts highlighted his sincerity. He was so concerned about making other people feel comfortable and important that he did whatever was necessary to create that culture interpersonally. Rarely did people comment on the words he chose, but they always commented on the *feeling* or connection that he inspired in them.

So, before you get started on the precise wording to use, focus on the concept of making a connection. I mentioned a few *Say This* phrases. Here are some *Not*

That statements that automatically disconnect you from the other party:

> Not *That*
>
> 1. I can't relate.
> 2. You're wrong.
> 3. How can you think that?
> 4. Judgments:
>   a. That's ridiculous.
>   b. I don't see it that way.
>   c. You're confused.

As a final example, let's consider what happens in families all the time. We all know how hard parents work on their connections with their kids in the interest of raising them well. I remember one father talking about the approach he took to managing the upbringing of his young boy. He wanted his son to have a morally upright perspective on the plethora of sexy images shouting from magazine racks and the media. If a provocative image appeared as they were standing in line at a grocery story or watching a TV show together, the father remembered what his own parents had said to him in the same situation: "That's disgusting!" He remembered what had gone through his own mind at the time: "Well dad, we must be different. I think it's appealing. I guess your generation is different than mine. Everyone likes that stuff now."

So the father tried a different approach. He knew that a young boy would find such images appealing to look at. So instead he would say, "Wow, that will catch your eye, won't it? It's difficult to look past that, isn't it?" This approach immediately connected him to the boy, because the boy could relate to that statement– it's what the boy was thinking, even though he didn't really want to say it. Then the father went on to explain why, despite the appeal of the images, it was wrong to look at women as objects. He shared his thoughts and made his point effectively. His intuition made the conversations easier to have.

Luckily, not every conversation you have with someone else will be as difficult as that one! But wherever you find yourself, do what you can to build or create a connection. Then you'll increase your allowable margin for error in words to an infinite degree. Of course, while connection is crucial, it isn't everything. Sooner or later, you still need to fill your conversations with as many of the right things as you can. Let's look at more *Say This* examples now.

❧ *Two* ❧

DISCOVER THE THREE-LEGGED STOOL

ONE OF THE MOST important ideas in getting your message across is the three-legged stool. A stool with one or two legs will fall, but a stool with at least three legs can stand without wobbling. Similarly, there are three points that will keep you in *Say This* mode when you communicate. When entering into any dialogue or monologue, remember to do the following:

1. **Be purposeful** before entering into an interaction with anyone, ready to serve the other person.

2. No matter how difficult it may be, make an attempt to **build the relationship**. (There are very rare occasions when this is not relevant – see below.)

3. Be **dignified** in your approach, remaining emotionally in-bounds and respectful.

Let's look more closely at each of these three key legs.

Be Purposeful

Many coaches and motivational speakers have written about the need to be purposeful. This idea is sometimes criticized because it sometimes sounds like license to manipulate the other person, using others to get what you want, even at their expense. And some books, such as *The Art of Seduction* and *The 48 Laws of Power*, deserve that criticism. But as I mentioned earlier, I'm writing with the assumption that you are interested in doing the right thing. There is a way to be purposeful without being cold and calculating.

To see this more clearly, think about the ways you want others to treat you. When you interact with a person you love, do you want him or her to be purposeful about making you feel loved? Of course you do. When you interact with your financial advisor, don't you want him to be purposeful about making sure you understand your financial situation? Indeed you do. Both personal and business-oriented circumstances require a strong sense of purpose, otherwise they become a waste of time for everyone.

A common *Not That* mistake is for people to confuse their subjects. You've probably been on the receiving end of this yourself. Think of a time you've spoken with someone who left you scratching your head wondering, "What's their point?" Sometimes, if you ask the person what their point is, they ramble even more, leaving you even more bewildered. This often happens when a person is intellectually unclear about his purpose for speaking. He may know on an emotional level but can't articulate it because he has not yet moved the message from his heart to his head.

I see this confusion a lot. When a start-up company asks me to take a consulting role, I ask the potential clients to describe the product or service they are offering. Quite often, I make my decision to accept the contract based on whether I can understand the company's objective from a simple sentence or two. I have found that if the founders or inventors of the concept can't communicate their objectives succinctly, then I will probably find myself having the same difficulty. Sometimes they contact me in the first place with the goal of making their products more marketable. But if I can't easily understand their purpose, I will usually walk away from the project.

In most cases, knowing your objective or purpose has nothing to do with becoming smarter. It's much simpler than that and relates to actions we take every day. You would never leave home unless you knew why you'd left and, in most cases, where you were going. Even if your purpose is merely to get some fresh air while aimlessly strolling, you've given it some forethought, and anyone who might see you out for a walk senses this – your actions make sense to them.

In communication, having a purpose means the same thing—knowing your destination. It helps you know when the conversation is over or when it needs to continue. It helps you get back on track, stay focused, or determine that your objective will not be met. It is like the part of a GPS that says, "at the next opportunity, make a legal U-turn," or "when possible make a right-hand turn."

Here are some examples of everyday purpose statements. These are not words you would say out loud, but reasons that shape what you are about to say.

1. To make you feel loved

2. So you understand why I did what I did ...

3. In order to make you feel comfortable in this new environment

4. So you understand the company philosophy

5. To prevent you from doing that same behavior the next time around

6. To laugh with you in order to build a greater connection

7. To reveal my heart to you to build trust and a further connection

8. To apologize for my actions

9. To show you that I care

10. To sell you the product that meets your needs

Build the Relationship

Depending on how you were raised or your temperament, this second leg of the three-legged stool might be hard for you to accept. Ever since Hippocrates introduced the world to the temperaments thousands of years ago, psychologists, business leaders, spiritual guides, and researchers have found them to be important tools for understand different human types.

On one side of the spectrum, some people are *phlegmatics.* They are naturally gifted in building relationships. That is, of course, an important skill to possess, but if unregulated, it may come at the cost of compromising personal integrity. It is easy to slip into valuing a relationship more than someone's purpose.

On the other side of the spectrum are *cholerics*, who are inclined to achieve their purpose even at the cost of relationships. Their intentions may be honorable – for example, they might have a strong sense of duty—but their desire to win can come at too great of a cost.

Thank God for such people. At times, there are extreme circumstances that call us to fight for a cause even if it means harming relationships and burning bridges. The courage of cholerics works well in such situations. Those circumstances are so rare, however, that they are not of concern in this book, and we will focus on building relationships while still obtaining your purpose.

When you disagree with someone but want to build the relationship, you don't need to abandon your principles, no matter how tense the situation becomes. Think of parents who correct their children in a firm tone while at the same time communicating love. Some of the most trusted and beloved coaches, teachers, and military leaders work very hard to uphold principles and build relationships at the same time.

The connection discussed in the previous chapter is often made possible by using all three legs. Like the coach who gives his team a scolding at halftime, you can deliver a message that is not pleasant if your purpose is morally sound. Trust can be built – your hearers know and value your intention.

The use of proper validation allows you to maintain a connection. It is like building a literal bridge. The stronger the bridge, the more weight it can carry. Likewise, sometimes the weight of the issue makes the communication process unpleasant, but if you've already built a strong connection, both parties can withstand the unpleasant nature of the conversation.

When you know you are entering a difficult conversation, consider using these phrases.

Say This

1. "On one hand, I understand what you have been going through and why you have conducted yourself the way you have. On the other hand, you and I both know that a change needs to take place. I want to be clear about what those changes are so we can move forward."

2. "This might feel personal, but I want you to know that I respect you. I am able to distinguish between the behaviors that need to change and who you are as a person. I hope you can see it that way as well."

3. "I am going to talk to you about some difficult things, but I want you to feel secure as we speak because I support you. I need to discuss this with you to get us back on track."

4. "I'd rather just let this topic go in order to keep peace, but I care enough about you that I need to bring it up. I hope you understand I am only discussing it because I care and respect you."

5. [In a very difficult case.] "My fear is that this topic will divide us. I really don't want that to happen because I value our relationship and want it to continue to grow. However, I must address this because there needs to be a change in this very important area…"

Not That

1. "Don't take this personally, but…" [followed by some reference to the person's character or essence]. You are better off having them take personal things personally than trying to pretend that it is not personal. A better alternative is *Say This* #2 above.

2. "To be honest with you…" This phrase is commonly used, but as we discuss elsewhere, it should be avoided because it sounds like you have lied to them before and may lie to them again, but at least for now you will be honest.

3. "I don't know why you do what you do, but it needs to change." Although this is not the worst *Not That* phrase, it begins with a disconnection, which makes the rest of your work very difficult.

4. "I can't believe you [did thus and so]…" This phrase unnecessarily risks a disconnect.

Quite likely, if you're a "tough" leader, you see some of these *Say This* phrases as ways of sugarcoating difficult situations. I can understand that perspective. Even in my own work, there have been times when I needed to make serious changes with certain people, and the approach I took was short and direct. It carried very little prefacing and, if you heard me, you might think I was ignoring my own advice. The difference is that in those situations, a relationship already existed, so a connection was there to stabilize the words.

Be Dignified

This third leg of the stool is crucial because it is the emotional regulator of the entire process. When we have conversations with others that are emotionally charged (positively or negatively), we can easily lose our self-respect. This can cause a disconnect with the other party.

One way to avoid this is to maintain an emotional "evenness" with the other party. To illustrate this, let's consider a *Not This* example. Have you ever been at a meeting where a motivational speaker is invited to come in, and as soon as he hits the stage he yells at the crowd, "Are you fired up? I didn't hear you! Are you fired up? Louder!" That might be acceptable in a sales meeting, but there are some groups that simply cannot relate to that abrupt message. For many people, myself included, it feels more like someone shouting in your face to wake you up. It might wake you up, but at the cost of feeling some disdain for the other party.

As a professional speaker, I often have a motivational slant to my messages. I have found that the best approach is to meet the audience where they are emotionally and then lead them into an enthusiastic state. Forcing it does not work well if there is not a previous connection. To keep the connection, begin with a normal tempo, volume, and energy level that builds as you progress. Likewise, during one-on-one conversations, match the other party's emotional state in order to establish a connection. This connects them to you, but because of your alertness and awareness, it also keeps you regulated by engaging your intellect and your emotions. It is always valuable to measure the possible reactions to certain emotions so that, if you sense that you are unintentionally sending the wrong message, you can alter your words and approach.

Other emotional disconnects occur when one party is so upset that he is beside himself with anger or hate. Yelling and hostile facial and postural cues repel listeners. Sometimes the opposite effect can occur, and an unhealthy level of passivity is displayed which can also lead to a disconnection.

Overall, the term *emotional evenness* means being equal to the other party's emotions as best you can. Keep in mind that there are times when it's appropriate to raise your voice, take on a defensive posture, or use carefully selected strong language. There are times when you will intentionally step outside of the other person's emotions to make your point. For example, a parent disciplining their child might intentionally express firmness that is intended to show the child the severity of a circumstance. But if that is unregulated and just happens without thinking, later on the parent often regrets yelling or being too firm. For the most part, emotional evenness is beneficial for building a connection. We have a difficult time hearing a message when we are distracted by other people's emotions.

The second component to this leg relates to our overall moral code. That requires us to avoid things that can damage a relationship, such as lying, yelling (unless it is absolutely necessary, like a coach trying to get his players' attention), using foul language, or presenting ourselves in any way that is inconsistent with who we are or what we stand for.

As I'm sure you know from experience, it is difficult to listen to someone you consider to be a hypocrite. Hypocrisy comes out not just when the person talks about principles different from his actions, but even when he communicates an important message in a less-than-dignified way. When you perceive that someone lacks dignity, you lose respect for them and experience disconnect

Part Two
SAY THIS,
NOT THAT ...

❧ *Three* ❧

TO SLAY THE CONVERSATION KILLERS

B<small>Y THIS POINT</small> you've probably noticed that the top conversation killers are related to anything that destroys an existing connection or prevents a connection in the first place. There are four primary conversations killers that will thwart your efforts to make a connection, even if you say all the right things.

o   Drifting off topic

o   Interrupting the other party

o   Not listening attentively

o   Lacking interest

Let's look at how you can slay these conversation killers.

Stay On-Topic

In a small gathering of executives, a Senior Vice-President of Sales began a discussion about an administrative policy. He was diplomatic in his presentation but clearly was frustrated with the current guidelines and described the situation using words such as "draconian." Before he was able to conclude, the chief administrator of the policy jumped in and said, "Of course, we have to do that—the sales field doesn't respect any of our policies so we need to reinforce them with penalties in order to get what we want." The VP was genuinely puzzled and in annoyance replied, "What are you talking about?" These words triggered emotions in the administrator, and he began a long irrelevant rant about various rules and regulations that had nothing to do with the sales field. In response to the VP's growing look of perplexity, the administrator fired off five different accusations of the sales field so rapidly that it was nearly impossible to respond to them. Within the matter of 60 seconds, their conversation had nothing to do with the original point. After it zigzagged for about ten unfruitful minutes, the only outcome was fresh wounds on top of previous scar tissue.

Whether or not you've ever been in this type of meeting, I'm sure you've had the experience of trying to share a concern, only to have the person you're talking with say something like, "that reminds me of…" Before you know it, you're talking about her ideas and you never even had a chance to get to the point you wanted to make. This leads to frustration, which can cause emotional flare-ups and a disconnect between parties. When that happens, it's important for you to skillfully steer the conversation back on track. This can be particularly difficult if the conversation is based on a need to correct the other person's actions or if it in any way conjures up feelings of insecurity. Those issues often cause the other party to become defensive and to try to deflect your "accusations."

Consider these *Say This, Not That* solutions:

Say This

1. "That's interesting, Joe. I can see why the topic reminds you of that. (*At this point continue with your point by using a segue such as:*) In fact..., Actually... That reminds me..."

2. "I'd like to hear more about that later..." (*Then confidentially continue with your point.*)

3. "I understand that is important to you. Can we discuss it after I share just a few more thoughts?"

4. If the other party is defensive and deflects the point by changing the topic, say, "I see what you're saying; however, it's actually not about that. It's about..." (*Then confidently get back to the point you were making. In other words, don't respond to their deflection by answering it. Finish the point you were addressing and then, if it is appropriate, turn to their point after you are finished.*)

5. "...However..." (This is generally a good word to introduce a different perspective. The *Not This* version is the word "but"—see below.)

Not That

1. "Excuse me, but I was saying..."

2. "You totally changed the topic on me..."

3. "You interrupted me..."

4. "Can I finish my point?"

5. "I'd like to hear more about that, but..." (Notice this is exactly like point 2 above, except that it includes the word "but.")

6. "...But..."

You'll notice that the *Say This* phrases don't have any accusation. On the other hand, the *Not That* phrases highlight the other party's error and may be interpreted as a personal attack. It is common sense that if you accuse people who are already becoming defensive, they will often raise their level of defensiveness and become more committed to gaining control of the conversation by changing the topic.

It's important for you to choose words that communicate understanding and empathy. This can be very difficult when, emotionally, you don't feel empathetic. But remember that there are two types of empathy: intellectual and emotional. At times we instantaneously have an emotionally empathetic connection to people. Those are usually the times when we say to ourselves, "I can relate." At other times, we lack that emotional connect, so we need to relate intellectually by placing ourselves in the other person's shoes. The key here is to say, "If I were *entirely* that person, I could imagine feeling and acting the same way he does." This is different from saying, "If that happened to me" or "If I was in that situation." Possibly, if you (as you are now) were in that situation, you would not feel the way they do. The key to intellectual empathy is to completely put yourself in their shoes, as them, not you.

When someone changes a topic it is usually because she objects to your point or has not received it with the interest or concern you would like her to have. You certainly cannot make others accept your point or care about it, but you can give your best effort towards influencing them in those directions. Using a cycle of conversation that I call path finding, you can regain control of a conversation and get back on track. The cycle looks like this:

1. You establish the topic and attempt to make your point.

2. The other party changes the topic.

3. You show empathy or agree in theory by making a connection: "I understand..." "I can see your point..." "That makes sense..."

4. Now you "reset the table." This means to use a brief reminder to come back to the original point. Then you make your request, summarize your objective, or state your expectations.

Notice that *Say This* phrases never include the word "but." "But" is understood as discrediting whatever precedes it. It is usually a connection killer. At times it may seem nearly impossible to avoid the word. If you must use it, try to emphasize the other person's point and deemphasize "but". Even better, I would encourage you to replace it with "however." This excellent word can be used to invalidate, but its softer connotation allows the other person to consider that you are simply highlighting an additional perspective.

If you fail to use the 3rd step of showing empathy and simply go back to your point, you will sometimes find that the other party will accuse *you* of changing the topic. How ironic that feels! Once you've regained control of the topic, it's important to reset the table. Be brief, otherwise people might become irritated at the repetition.

Don't Interrupt the Other Party

Everyone has a different level of tolerance for being interrupted. No matter what your level is, at some point, you'll find it irritating. But inevitably, we do it to others as well. Sometimes we do it because we misinterpret their pause as the completion of a thought or an invitation to speak. Other times, we interrupt because we believe our interjection will be useful. Finally, we interrupt because we can no longer tolerate the words we're hearing, and we want to take control to prevent further frustration.

The bottom line, though, is that most interruptions are rude, increase agitations, and create division. The problem is that they are nearly impossible to avoid. We all speak with slightly different cadences, thought processes, socialized expectations, temperaments, and knowledge, and this creates a environment where we will inevitably make this mistake from time to time. So here are some *Say This, Not That* ways to handle interruptions when you're interrupted and when you are the one interrupting.

When you are interrupted:

Say This

1. "I can see you're eager (ready) to share your perspective (ideas, thoughts). I'd like to hear them in a minute…" (*then continue confidently with your point*).

2. "That's interesting (that makes sense)…" Then continue with your point.

3. "We should talk about that. In the meantime…"

When you are the one who has interrupted and you realize your error:

> *Say This*
>
> 1. "I'm sorry, that was rude. I thought you were finished. Go on. I'm listening."
> 2. "I didn't mean to do that. I'm sorry. Please finish."

When someone interrupts you:

> *Not That*
>
> 1. "You interrupted me..." (The same logic as when the topic is changed by the other party.)
> 2. "Can I finish?" (Same as above)
> 3. "That's rude. I'm not done."
> 4. "How dare you?"
> 5. Raise your voice to be heard over the other party

When you interrupt someone else:

> *Not That*
>
> 1. (Defensively) "Well, I thought you were finished."
> 2. "I want to talk too, you know."
> 3. "When do I get my turn?"
> 4. "I already get your point!"
> 5. "What's the big deal? I'm just making my point too."

Interruptions are a key source of frustration. Surprisingly, this is seen and felt more in intimate relationships than in professional settings. For some reason, many of us can tolerate interruptions from colleagues but not from our loved ones. At work, we keep our professional disposition, which ensures a calmer, more understanding reaction to interruptions. But our loved ones can sometimes push buttons, creating a different, less controlled response.

The most important takeaway on interruptions is to *be patient*. Wait it out. Let the other party finish his thought or sentence before you interject or reply. Even if you were the one originally interrupted, you still should follow that formula. Let the interrupter finish the thought, and then regain control. Although it may feel like an injustice to let them have the floor, doing this is the best course of action. Pointing out the interruption and asking for the right to finish can work, but only for some people. Even if you know the other party well and recognize that they are able to handle a kind yet more direct statement, it's always a good idea to soften your words. "I'm sorry Kathy, I'd like to hear that—however, do you mind if I just finish this thought first?"

Listen Attentively

I'll never forget the feeling I had after a highly regarded college professor paid me a very kind compliment. It felt personal and sincere. That all changed some years later, after I stood next to him at an event where we both gave speeches. I noticed that he provided the identical compliment to each person with whom he had a brief interaction. I realized he was acting with the same reflexes an insincere husband uses when he mechanically repeats phrases such as "Yes, dear" and "I'm sorry you feel that way." He doesn't actually consider what his wife has on her mind. That professor's words were merely a way to gain favor with people, but they had all the depth of a dinner plate.

He had become skilled enough to know what words would give the impression that he was paying attention and being sincere. Because my line of work is social, I'm empathetic to the stress that comes with meeting many people and at times feeling self-conscious that I should be remembering faces or names that I might have forgotten. It's easy to hide behind certain phrases that are sure to generate positive feelings in others. Unfortunately, this practice isn't effective in the long term because people begin to identify cookie cutter phrases over time. Thoughtful personalized commentaries signify sincerity and should be used whenever it is possible.

There is no need to describe what it feels like to talk to someone who doesn't pay attention to what you're saying. It may be necessary for me to remind you, however, that other people feel the same way when you don't pay attention to them. Most of us have a tendency to give ourselves too much credit when it comes to our listening skills, while at the same time demanding high standards from the people we talk to.

The three main reasons that people fail to listen attentively are: distraction, thinking about what they want to say in reply, and lack of interest in the topic.

Distraction

If you find yourself distracted in a conversation, it's smart to acknowledge the distraction instead of pretending it didn't happen. It's helpful to say something like, "I'm sorry, Bob. I was distracted. That was rude. I want to give you the attention this deserves. What was the last part of what you said?" People are generally quite forgiving about this the first time. Be careful to pay attention after that point, though, because even the best wording won't make up for a second offense in the same conversation.

If you find that you're so distracted you can't pay attention at that time, request a different time to talk. This is something I often find necessary to do during busy or stressful times. Say something like, "Terry, do you mind if we set up a time to talk about this in more detail? This is an important topic and I want to give you and it my full attention. But right now, I'm working on a project that is distracting me from doing that. Can we talk tomorrow at 2 p.m. so I'm fully prepared to listen?" You can adapt this basic idea to fit the nature of the relationship and the urgency of the issue.

If you find that you are communicating with someone who is distracted, here are some *Say This, Not That* phrases to keep in mind:

Say This
- "Ann, I could be wrong, but it seems like I caught you at a time where you have something on your mind. Can we talk another time? I really want to share this at a time that is convenient for you."

Not That

- "Ann, you seem distracted. Will you please pay attention?"

The key idea in this situation is to avoid passing blame or making the other person feel defensive. Most likely, if she is distracted, she is under stress. It could be positive stress (like preparing for a vacation) or negative stress (like being worried about losing a job). Either way, when you accept responsibility for the timing, you'll find in most cases that the other person will immediately recognize your graciousness and reply with something like, "No, no. I'm sorry. I was distracted but now is good. I'm ready to listen. Go ahead."

If you imply an accusation, you might hear Ann say the same words, but she will now be even more distracted by the fact that she feels accused. So even though you get her to acknowledge the distraction, she may not be paying more attention. Instead she just might hide the distraction more skillfully and go into auto-pilot with canned phrases that can emulate actual attentiveness.

I realize not everyone responds in these ways. Some people will sincerely accept the responsibility and own the distraction. But if we could rely on the virtues of the other party to solve the problems of communicating we would rarely have problems. Great communicators speak to the weaknesses, insecurities, and vices of their subjects without making them feel accused or small in any way.

Of course, there is a time and a place for people in authority to call a spade a spade and tell others directly what they think about their behaviors. Difficult conversations have a place. But in 99% of the cases, you can find ways to be gentler in your wording.

Thinking about what you are going to say
before the other person is finished talking

Many people condemn this practice in a wholesale fashion. I find that to be unfair because preparing what you are going to say is often involuntary. In fact, it's my experience that this practice is actually the *best* way to communicate—as long as it is managed within certain guidelines. For example, it is important to think about your reply in the context of what the other person is saying. It is only when you shut out your subject and disregard her input that thinking ahead becomes ineffective.

But the argument about whether or not this is a right or even effective practice is moot because it's nearly impossible for some people to change this innate behavior. God gave certain people the ability to process information quickly and effectively, allowing them to pay attention and formulate next steps. Others are not blessed in that way. They may have the gift of laser focus on the other person's thoughts and feelings. Both types of people can claim attentiveness in their own way. Therefore, asking either party to depart from their nature is ineffective.

It is, however, effective and important to practice courtesies in order to communicate attentiveness. When you are listening, keep eye contact and don't interrupt. These two things will allow you to think about your reply and still communicate attentiveness. And if you really want to take the conversation to the next level, repeat back part of what they said when it is time for you to talk.

Say This: "Tony, I hear you and understand when you say that... In light of that, what do you think about ..."

Not That: "Tony, what do you have to say about...?"

Tony might be looking for confirmation that you heard his previous point before you move to the next point. Acknowledgment is related to validation and is every bit as important. Notice the *Say This* wording, including repeating back what Tony said in summary form while using it as the platform to launch the next topic. "In light of that" demonstrates that you are building on the previous parts of the conversation and not simply moving topics around or jumping from point to point.

If you find your subject thinking about what he wants to say before you complete your point, you can try these *Say This, Not That* ideas:

Say This

- After completing your idea, end with a question based on your thought such as this. "Based on that, what specific insights or thoughts come to mind? If you don't mind being specific, I'd appreciate it because I value your insights about the point I just made."

Not That

- "You aren't even paying attention, are you? It looks like you're just ready to say what you want to say, and you're not even listening."

As right in principle as you may be in the *Not That* example, you'll never win this battle. That sort of statement rarely produces the response or actions you're hoping for. The *Say This* example, on the other hand, has no accusation and directs the behavior you desire by making your expectation clear and complimenting the other person. It is a connection maker, not a connection breaker.

Take an Interest in the Topic

At some point, you've had the experience of engaging in a conversation with someone who is enthusiastically sharing information about a topic in which you had no interest. We've all been there, just as we've all been the ones going on and on about something our listener really doesn't care about. In that setting, though, some people can make you feel like your boring topic is the most interesting thing they've ever heard. How and why are they able to do that? Is it sincere, or just a shallow strategy like the one used by the professor I mentioned earlier? Most often, people who do this effectively are so interested in the person sharing that the specific topic is not all that relevant.

In other words, they are actively engaged in what the topic means *to the other party*, so their enthusiastic or attentive replies don't depend on their own interest in the topic. They are tied to the person. These people have a true gift of attentiveness. Not everyone can demonstrate that gift equally effectively. Despite that, however, there are other things that all of us can do and say in this setting. When it comes to what to do, try the following:

1. Keep eye contact
2. Listen

3. Remember that what matters is not that you are interested in the topic. It's that you are interested in the person and relate to her feelings about the topic.

Here are some *Say This, Not That* scenarios:

Say This

1. "Wow, is that as exciting for you as it sounds?"

2. "How does being involved in that make you feel?"

3. "Tell me more about that."

4. "What's that like?"

5. "What's next for you on that (topic)?"

Not That

1. "I have no interest in that topic, but I see it's important to you."

2. "I can't relate because I don't play soccer (ride horses, read those kinds of books, have money to travel to those places, etc.)"

3. "You actually like that...?"

4. "Wow, neat."

5. "That's exciting" (usually followed by looking away and ending the conversation).

Here again, the key here is to build bridges, not tear them down. The *Say This* suggestions show interest but allow you the flexibility of not knowing anything about the topic. They inquire in a way that lets the subject explore the topic further, on her own terms. With these statements, the interest you show is in the person, so they are rarely misinterpreted as insincere.

The first three *Not That* replies are all divisive in some way. They may leave the person feeling disconnected or even defensive about her interests. The last two examples are often used by people who recognize the importance of making a connection but use words that lack depth and leave the conversation flat. There is a mixed message when you say that something is "exciting", but then you either desire to end the conversation or have nothing more to add. These statements can communicate the opposite of what the words mean if additional questions or statements fail to back them up. The *Say This* examples do not risk this because they shift the conversation back to the other person and give them the chance to keep talking about the topics they enjoy.

❧ *Four* ❧

TO RAISE STANDARDS

As I MENTIONED in the introduction, I am writing from the perspective of leadership in organizational settings. The next several chapters are oriented to specific circumstances to make the practical applications apparent. I think you will find insights on the perspective of a subordinate. It is my goal to pick scenarios that are easily translatable to most relationships, including peer relationships. As a coach, leader of executives, and trainer I know that leadership is a very popular subject. In fact, I offer coaching programs on the subject that I call the "Push/Pull of Leadership." As the title suggests, the purpose of the program is to help leaders understand that there are times to push and times to pull. In other words, there is a time to challenge and a time to nurture.

Helping people raise their standards takes more than having high standards yourself. It includes managing sensitivities, egos, and politics. It would be nice if we could just tell people, "pick up your performance." Simple, encouraging phrases do exist, and in the most basic situations they can be applied. There are times where these *Say This* phrases work just fine:

Say This

1. Let's pick things up, team.

2. You need to raise the bar—now get it going.

3. You've been under-performing. I expect more out of you.

4. Get it moving, or else… (*In rare situations, this is appropriate.*)

This direct wording is effective in one of three situations. The first is when the authority you have over someone is unquestioned and the penalty for underperforming is apparent and undesirable (or the reward for increasing performance is apparent and appealing). Two such situations are the military and athletics.

The second is if a connection is already established and a strong bond of trust is already present. The third scenario is when the person under authority is independently motivated. He wants to either avoid failure or achieve success, and such a person is motivated from within, so he basically ignores ridicule and encouragement by existing authority.

But those are the easy cases. If you're in one of those scenarios, you really don't need anything more than visceral instincts to drive up standards. In more delicate situations, skill is important. Here are a few situations that require additional ability:

- Raising standards of highly talented and marketable employees, while keeping them happy in the work environment.

- Raising standards when self-esteem issues are apparent in your subject.

- Raising standards when the subject is a perennial underachiever, yet the only person available to work with, such as in a volunteer setting.

- When the relationship is very new but higher standards are urgent right away (such as taking over the leadership role in a struggling organization).

- Raising standards when the low standards were embarrassing in some way. Standards that resulted in scandals or costly mistakes would be examples of this.

Leadership requires strength, but it also requires nuance. It is essential for leaders to have the strength to make the right calls ethically, morally, and even strategically, no matter how unpopular the decision might be. Sometimes it is clear that no matter how carefully you word a resolution, people will rebel. In those situations, it will be strength more than skill that will allow you to survive and thrive. But in most cases, the way in which you frame things will determine whether your words elicit severely negative reactions or produce positive reactions.

In this chapter, instead of looking at a number of different examples, let's follow one story, a practical example from real life. My client Dan was a newly assigned leader whose task was to raise standards for an underperforming group. Dan had no history with the group, so he needed to build rapport and establish trust. His primary asset was a track record of success that was impressive enough for his team to trust his professional opinion. He was briefed by the president of the company and told "there are some egos you'll need to take care of."

Dan did a number of smart things. He asked questions and listened before making any changes. He wanted to "take the temperature" of the staff. He now had seven people directly reporting to him, and he supervised an organization of 200. He quickly discovered that those who reported directly to him had substantially different perspectives on the company's past and future. They also had differing ideas about Dan on a personal level. What they did share was a mood of concern. Five of the seven were afraid of losing their jobs, and the other two were so fed up they seemed not to care either way. A lack of self-confidence was the overarching issue.

Among other things Dan discovered that his predecessor, Tom, had anticipated being replaced by Dan, so he went to great lengths to undermine Dan prior to his arrival. Dan speculated that Tom did this in order to justify his own failures after he was fired. Whatever the motivation, it was an ugly situation. Tom had privately attacked Dan's character on a personal level with false accusations. On a professional level, he also attacked Dan by discrediting his successes. It was corporate politics in its lowest form.

Dan had the ultimate task ahead of him. He needed to raise standards quickly while managing a campaign to tarnish his authority and credentials. First, he made a decision to never speak poorly of Tom in any situation. This was a great *Not That* move. Second, he keyed in on the lack of confidence he recognized in his new team of seven. Here is the entire two-minute monologue. It's so rich with *Say This* wording that it is best to read it as a whole and then break it down later.

He opened his first meeting with these words:

"After speaking with all of you individually, I have a great sense of confidence that we will be able to make the changes we need to make in order to prosper. It's clear to me that the past results were not due to a lack of individual talent, as each of you is well suited for your role. While I'm not that interested in pointing fingers at anyone for the past, I know we need to confront mistakes head-on in order to avoid them in the future. That must be done, without blame and with an eye towards the future. The primary change that we need to make is one of culture. That will be all of our responsibilities. It cannot be done alone. We must all enthusiastically support each other's individual efforts in order to grow as a whole. Some of you may not like that idea. I hope that is not the case. I personally have decided that this team, as it exists, is a team that can take us to great places, but you must each decide, on your own, whether or not you will fit in here. There is no shame in deciding to move on if you choose to. That would not reflect on you professionally or personally. A glove is still a glove, even if it does not fit every hand.

"I would like to tell you a story of failure. Twelve years ago, I was assigned to my first leadership role at this level. I was called to lead the East Region. We made so many mistakes together. The first nine months of that assignment, I feared a pink slip on a daily basis. I made personnel mistakes and strategic mistakes. Despite a great team of people, we went backwards for the first year. That experience was the best thing that ever happened to me as a leader. I was given a dose of humility, which I have learned is the biggest tool in the toolbox of leadership. Some of you know the rest of the story. We were blessed with tremendous prosperity and grew the region more than any region in company history, but that came after a very dark year. I'm grateful that the board did not give up on me during my struggle. I force myself to remember that feeling each day as a leader."

"Today, I speak to you as the Vice President of this department, but I also speak to you as a mutual member of this team. You are leaders, and I see you that way. You are here at this meeting not to be reminded that you report to someone else but to be reminded of the importance of the leadership role you play. These meetings are your meetings. They are going to be designed to empower you with the tools you need to get your work done. We will sometimes disagree at this table. We will sometimes win arguments, lose arguments, concede points or fight harder to make a point. But all of that must be done for the purpose of building up, not tearing down. It must be done with humility and confidence, strength and meekness. In other words, it must be done out of concern for the team and not out of a desire for personal ambition."

"Your past mistakes are not F's on a report card; they were internships, which prepared you for this hour. You are all very valuable, and together we will build something great. Let's establish a culture of confidence, hard work, loyalty, and, without question, results. We will get results. We begin now."

There are three major themes that Dan carried through his message. They are all important when trying to raise standards.

- Security
- Defining of issues (statement of future standards)
- Autonomy to choose whether or not to be part of the team.

Establish Security

Dan's comments show his awareness of security. He kept, front and center in his mind, the fact that five of the seven were concerned about their jobs. Most managers would play on employees' fear of losing their jobs in order to motivate them to work harder. It's easy to understand why. No doubt, people will perform in order to provide for their families. But people will also lie, cheat, and steal when no trust is present and they face "or else" scenarios, even if the "or else" is subtle. Even though many people rise to the occasion during difficult times, others become so weakened emotionally that they begin to act like completely different people.

Prior to engaging with his new team, Dan was prepared to terminate any team member he found to be unqualified, so his assessment of this team as qualified to turn the business around was sincere. It was wise of him to state this reality publically in order to reduce tensions, raise confidence, and hopefully get a reciprocal commitment from them. Notice that Dan doesn't just say something like, "at this point I have decided that you're all going to keep your jobs." This is a classic *Not That* way of managing this circumstance. It assumes that one statement is enough and that merely saying people will keep their jobs makes them feel secure. That is assurance, but in difficult times people need *re*-assurance. So saying it in more than one way is important. He planted several reassuring statements throughout his message:

1. ...each of you is well suited for your role.

2. ...without blame

3. ...this team, as it exists, is a team that can take us to great places...

4. Your past mistakes are not F's ... You are all very valuable....

Besides these statements, Dan also told a story of personal failure in order to reassure the team that he understands mistakes and that he knows great things can happen even after much failure.

It's almost impossible to raise standards without trust. When standards are high enough, it usually means more work hours, mental (creative) effort, or physical effort. Very few people are willing to put more effort into something they can freely choose to leave unless they trust that the rewards will be worth the efforts. If you are a leader, then the trust is likely tied directly to you.

To a degree, Dan removed doubt about past mistakes, qualifications, and even future mistakes. All of these efforts allowed the team to lower their defenses.

That allowed Dan to get to know them for who they really were, with an eye toward reevaluating their performance later.

Define the Issues

Dan clearly defined the issues. When it comes to running a business, the key issues will need more specifics than a two-minute set of opening comments, but Dan framed them the following ways:

1. "We need to confront the mistakes head-on."

2. "The primary change that we need to make is one of culture. That will be all of our responsibility. It cannot be done alone."

3. "These meetings are your meetings. They are going to be designed to empower you with the tools that you need to get your work done."

4. "Let's establish a culture of confidence, hard work, loyalty and without question, results."

Dan went on to define the issues from an empirical perspective by providing the current productivity statistics and financials. He then established targets and obtained support for the new direction. A mistake that many communicators make is to jump right into the statistical changes that need to be made, without addressing the culture. Typically this produces disconnection in the boardroom. It is crucial to address the heart before the head in most circumstances. By defining the terms, Dan laid the foundation for inviting people to join him in facing new challenges. Rather than forcing anything on them, they remained free to choose what to do.

Offer Autonomy and Choice

The power to choose is the yeast in the bread of new standards—it makes them rise. The desire to have power to choose is a universally appealing need. Regardless of whether you are reading this book as a parent, partner, volunteer, or corporate leader, using these *Say This* choices will empower you. Unlike in other *Say This* lists in the book, you probably won't use these exact words, but you can definitely adapt Dan's words to your own situation.

Let's take a look at how Dan set this up:

1. "I personally have decided that this team, as it exists, is a team that can take us to great places but you must decide individually whether or not you will fit in here."

2. "There is no shame in deciding to move on if you choose to. That would not reflect on you professionally or personally. A glove is a glove, even if it does not fit every hand."

When people feel forced to make changes, they often resent the change, and their drive diminishes. You can observe this in entrepreneurs who leave jobs because their hours were dictated by others. They seek the freedom to choose to work when they want, where they want. In the end, many work more hours and earn less money than they did working for someone else. However, they would never change back to the old scenario because they "choose" to work the longer hours rather than being "made" to work certain hours without a voice in the matter.

This concept of needing to make a choice even applies to employees who are happy to work hours set by others. These employees know that it is their choice to work for that person. So instead of focusing on the lack of choice about hours, they look at the choice to quit or stay as their empowerment.

A large medical supplier and client of mine recently adapted the total flex schedule philosophy that companies like Best Buy have adopted, allowing their employees to work when they want, where they want. The result was increased job satisfaction and productivity, not to mention attracting great talent. It was interesting how people responded to the shift. Although the opportunity to make the change was to provide more choices for the employees, the reaction of some workers was to resist the freedom to choose since they wanted to make the choice to be free to choose! That demonstrates how deep this need is. We often want the freedom to choose things we really don't even have a right to choose. Choice drives markets and makes capitalism thrive, but it has limits.

Dan was clear that anyone could choose to leave and would not be judged if that was her decision. But if she chose to stay, the old attitude/culture needed to go. Dan gave his employees the freedom to choose to be on the team, but not to keep the old standards. You might hire a personal trainer to push you through workouts. If you choose the trainer, you would choose to do what he says, but if someone you did not know came up to you and ordered you to do push-ups, you would probably refuse. Choosing to work with a person or a situation makes all the difference. Within reason, it is best to use language that does not make people feel forced to do what you ask unless that is absolutely necessary. The more autonomy you give them to decide for themselves, the greater their commitment will be if they choose to make the change you are inviting them to make.

❧ *Five* ❧

TO BUILD TRUST

STEPHEN COVEY WROTE a great work called *The Speed of Trust*. The book's main message is that where there is trust, progress is made rapidly, but where there is no trust, progress is slow at best. Trust is essential, and words can accelerate or destroy trust. So when you want to build trust, getting the words right is important. Trust goes even deeper than the basic connection we've been discussing throughout this book. You can feel connected to people when you share interests with them, but you don't necessarily trust them. People at a party feel a connection with other partiers. They enjoy each other's company and connect on a certain level. But would that connection be enough to make a person share the keys to his new car? Or allow a fellow partygoer to babysit his kids? Not if there was no trust.

So how do you take a simple connection and turn it into trust? What are the right words? No words can mask repeated contradicting actions. Certainly a few falters here and there can be forgotten and corrected with words, but actions are presumed present with the trust wording I am about to provide. There are three stages in building trust with words.

1. Lower defenses
2. Speak their language
3. Provide assurances (*or terms, if no assurances are present*)

Lower defenses

When defenses are high, trust will not grow. The need to defend happens because trust is absent. Sometimes we have good reasons for not trusting people, other times we lack trust based on our intuition. And other times, we don't trust people because, for whatever reason, they don't trust us.

When it comes to trust, someone always has to make the first move. One of the best ways to do that is to use a tool we have already discussed: validation. Validating someone else's experiences will engender trust faster than anything else I have ever seen. I've seen untrustworthy people win over unsuspecting future victims by validating their experiences. Validation is so soothing to most people that it can make them lower their guards when it would be wiser to keep them up. Validation itself is a morally neutral tool that should be used with good intentions and not simply as a technique to get something.

Validation is a way to make the first move in establishing trust, but there's an even more direct way. That is to trust the other party "first" and to communicate to the other party that you trust her. Often, people get caught in a battle of wills and say things like "I don't trust you" or "Why should I trust you?" Certainly those statements can be justified at times, but they'll never lead to progress. Very few people are humble enough, or strong enough, to make the effort to try to regain the trust by trusting first. If you want to get things on the path of trust, you might need to be the one to make the first move.

Being accused of untrustworthiness is one of the hardest accusations for anyone to hear. Even when it is true, it strikes a chord that causes defensiveness in most people. When that happens, people will usually defend themselves by firing shots back. Suddenly, you can find yourself caught up in the loop of "Oh yeah, I don't trust you either. Remember when you…" or "How can I trust someone who…?"

Eventually both parties spend most of their time on why they can't trust each other, as opposed to identifying what they can use as common ground for trust. Of course, if you're going to trust first, you need to use a little prudence. Frivolously extending trust to someone who might harm you if they broke the trust would not be wise. Even if you had plenty of money, you would not give your 16-year-old the keys to your Ferrari and say, "Have fun. See you whenever you feel like coming home." But you would probably give him the keys to the minivan, ask where he is going, and tell him to be home by 10:00. Over time, you will trust him more.

What makes *trusting first* so effective is that when someone trusts us, most of us automatically warm up and decide to trust in them in return. Internally, we say to ourselves, "Well, I guess I should trust her, at least a little. After all, she trusts me, so she's got to have some good judgment."

Here are some ideas for building trust:

Say This

1. "I know it will take time for us to build trust." (Acknowledging the situation for what it is builds trust, because it's a statement of connection. You are just putting into words what the other party probably already feels.)

2. "I trust you to... [do something or hold something in confidence...]" (At whatever level makes sense.)

3. "Over time, I look forward to building our relationship. It feels like we'll be able to build trust." (This statement declares your desire and your early intuition without being unrealistic or fake. The other party may even accelerate their timetable of trust by reciprocating positive feelings.)

4. "I'd like to build trust, which is why I would like to share my credentials (resume, intentions, skills, track record)." (Building trust on a credential level is a good way to begin. It is a stronger practice than asking someone to trust based on good intentions.)

5. "I'd like to hear more about you." (Most forms of "tell me about yourself" are very effective. People trust good listeners. If they talk about themselves without being judged and with validation, trust will build rapidly.)

6. "I understand how you feel."

7. "That makes sense."

8. "I can see your point of view."

9. "That must be difficult."

10. "I am sorry to hear that."

Not That

1. "You can trust me." (Anyone can say that. This statement is weak from the start unless it is backed up with a reason. It is better to say, "I know you have no reason to trust me at this point, but I hope it helps to know that I am a… " [see example 4 above.)

2. "To tell you the truth." "Honestly." (This is subtle and often it is used as common filler, but be careful using it. It can leave the impression that you have lied to them before and you will lie again, but just for now you will tell them the truth.)

3. "I don't trust you." (You might not trust the other party, but telling them this is rarely effective for building trust. It is better to state things like, "in order for us to build trust, I'd like to see you [do, say, provide, etc.]…")

4. "Why should I trust you?" (This is not a terrible thing to say to all audiences, since some people will want to prove they are trustable, but it is not wise to use since most people will become defensive. They may try to turn this around and make you

prove why *they* should trust *you*. It can backfire easily.)

5. "What makes you think…?" (This sounds like a subtle judgment of their reasoning, akin to "What on earth makes you think…?" It's better to say, "How did you arrive at that perspective?")

6. Embellishments or lies of any kind.

7. Sarcasm. (Sends a message of incongruence that makes you hard to read. The listener thinks, "Did he mean that or not?")

8. Overt compliments or relationally inappropriate comments.

   a. "You look great today."

   b. "You are my favorite."

   c. "I'm such a big fan of yours."

Speak their Language

It's an axiom that people tend to like people like themselves. Even where opposites initially attract, it's usually only a matter of time before the differences that were once exciting eventually divide. Pay close attention to the word choices made by the other party, and use them where they are appropriate. You can take this too far by using words that are simply not in your verbal bank, of course. Then they may come off as unnatural unless you use a disclaimer such as, "to use your word, which I think really makes the point, it is 'exquisite.'" This compliments her word choice, demonstrates that you were listening, and puts you in agreement with her feelings.

This point is important because not only do people like people like themselves, but they tend to *trust* people like themselves. For example, people who are not naturally good at eye contact don't really care that others don't use eye contact. In fact, they're usually uncomfortable with people who say "look at me when you talk to me." It goes without saying that people who are naturally good at eye contact are uncomfortable with people who don't look them in the eyes. Building trust is heavily influenced by matching others' language and communications style as best you can.

Speaking another person's language can also mean using the same word "chunks": the amount of words to describe things or answer questions. Some people like hearing every detail and sharing every detail. If you are trying to build trust with such a person, then share all the details. Others just want headlines. If that is the case, just share headlines. Be yourself, but do it in a way that accommodates individual perspectives and tendencies.

The only note of caution I have is to do this within your comfort zone. If you try to become the other person rather than simply being yourself in a way that is accommodating, then you will be unnatural. This is a sure way to lose ground in building trust.

Provide Assurances

Not every interaction we have requires assurances. When there is no need for assurance, there is usually less of a need to establish a strong level of trust. But this section concerns the times where trust is essential for the relationship to prosper.

In the previous section I listed "Why should I trust you?" as *Not That* wording. I listed it because it can lead to a defensive response, thereby defeating efforts to build trust. It is, however, a legitimate question that each of us asks ourselves when we're in a new or strained relationship. You should expect that even if the other party doesn't ask the question out loud, she is still thinking it. So it makes sense to answer it if you can.

Tell the other party what you plan on doing if action is required. Only list things you will certainly do, otherwise you will break trust later. Failing to follow through will do substantial damage to the trust process.

Here are some examples.

Say This

1. "I am going to…" (Followed by anything you will be able to provide, avoid, or accommodate. If you can provide timelines and other details, this message is much more powerful.)

2. "I'm not sure if you're looking for assurance, but I'd like to provide some things that might put you at ease if you are." (If it is obvious that they are looking for assurance, leave out the "I'm not sure" part.)

3. "I will do my best to…" (Followed by things that can't be assured but are intended).

4. "I would like to assure you that… however, I can't be certain of it myself. I will work towards…"

(Say this when you have limited power to make changes but you are in agreement with the spirit of the request. Notice I left out the word "but" and replaced it with "however." As we saw earlier, this small change communicates a spirit of moving forward. The word "but" makes it sound more like you *want to* assure them, but you won't. "However" makes it sound like you want to assure them, and you will do so to the best of your ability.)

These statements validate the importance of taking action to satisfy another person's concerns. If you are willing to do something in order to accommodate another person's needs, she may assume that you are validating her needs, but that assumption should not be automatic. In an analogy I mentioned earlier a company measured customer satisfaction based on rectifying errors. Their internal score was an A, but the customers weren't impressed until the customer relation reps met them emotionally. Just stating an intended outcome as a matter of assurance can fall short. To ensure a connection, and therefore the seedbed of trust, try adding:

Say This

1. "Because you have had to go through that experience, I will…"

2. "I am sure that was difficult, so I would like to…"

3. "I am sorry to hear about that. I wish I could correct that, but I know I can't. I will do everything

> I can to fix what is fixable because you should not
> have had to deal with that…"
>
> 4.   "Wow, how exciting! I'm happy for you. In the
>   meantime I will…" (Not all trust situations are
>   negative. Sometimes, people decide to trust or not
>   to trust based on other interactions.)

Here are some phrases to avoid, as well as some alternatives.

> *Not That*
>
> 1.   "I can guarantee that you're wrong." (Yes, this
>   might be assurance, and you might in fact be right,
>   but better wording is, "I am 100% confident that
>   I have this information correct, but I will double-
>   check and send you the data so you can make
>   your own decision about it.")
>
> 2.   "You have my word." (This might work if
>   you have no history or good history, but not if you
>   have not honored your word in the past. If you
>   have not proven trustworthy this statement just
>   agitates or infuriates people.)

Real trust is the ultimate form of connection. It allows for tremendous flexibility in language. When we trust people, we tend to take what they say in the best light. When we don't trust them, we often read things between the lines that are never intended.

❧ *Six* ❧

TO HANDLE OTHER
SITUATIONS

To Apologize

THE DESIRE TO apologize is usually based on good intentions, but if you do it the wrong way, it's worse than if you had said nothing at all. We often see this in the news with politicians who offer apologies that only dig the hole deeper. In this section, I'll start with the *Not That* examples. These examples assume that you are dealing with bigger, more serious issues. If you're just apologizing for something like spilling milk, a simple "oops, I'm sorry" should suffice.

The need for a more elaborate apology comes about when you say something hurtful, act irresponsibly, or betray someone's trust. A more formal apology can also be necessary for acts that are less serious but still hurtful, such as being inconsiderate.

Not That

1. "I'm sorry. It's just that..." (followed by "I had to," "you made me," or anything else that sounds like you aren't accepting responsibility).

2. "I'm sorry, but why'd you have to…?" (Even if the other person bears some responsibility, it's best to keep that separate in the conversation. Remember, "but" is often heard as eliminating whatever positive statement was said previous to it.)

3. "Fine, I'll apologize. (*With attitude*) Sorry. Does that make you feel better?"

4. "I'm sorry it bothers you, but how can you blame me?" (When you are sorry only for the way someone feels and not the actions that caused the feelings, you are less effective. Sometimes, of course, you really aren't sorry for the actions, and this may be the best you can do. In this case, better wording is, "I'm sorry that this hurts your feelings. I wish I could avoid it. If I could find a better way I would, but under these circumstances this is the best I can do.")

5. "I'm sorry that you feel that way." (This is the classic bad apology. Even if you sincerely feel compassion for the other person, he will only hear this as condescending and patronizing. Avoid this sort of language.)

For an apology to have the greatest chance of inspiring forgiveness and renewed trust, it must contain three parts:

1. *Contrition.* You must display sorrow for the mistake. Words such as "I'm sorry" or "I apologize" are often all it takes if they are said with an appropriate sentiment.

2. *Accepting ownership.* You must communicate that you own your part in the infraction, without passing blame. "It was my fault." "I did it through my own weakness." "I'm embarrassed by the fact that it was my fault." Even when you know you aren't responsible for the entire infraction, it's best to keep that part separate from your apology, even if the separation is only a matter of minutes. If you later need to point out fault that is not your own, be careful to separate it from your own role as best you can, so it does not sound like you are trying to take back your apology or minimize how much you made a mess of things.

3. *Assurance.* "I will do everything in my power to avoid it in the future," or, if it makes sense in the situation, "It will never happen again." (Refer to the chapter on trust to see more on assurance.)

So ultimately, the best apology covers these three main points:

Say This

1. "I'm sorry."

2. "It was my fault."

3. "I will do everything I can to avoid it happening in the future."

The hardest part of apologizing has nothing to do with words and everything to do with will. Pride gets in the way of most people saying these things, so here is a suggestion. Remember that an incomplete apology will usually never get you what you want in the first place. Most of the time, even people who are motivated only to apologize halfway really do want to restore the relationship—otherwise they wouldn't go through the effort in the first place. So apologize fully out of self-interest as well as nurturing good business relations. A half-hearted apology is like buying an airline ticket that gets you halfway to your destination. You don't want to be tossed out of the plane at 35,000 feet. A half apology feels good at first, but never lands you safely. So go all out with your apologies.

When you don't have time to prepare

Life is full of surprises. Being caught off-guard and not knowing what to say is one of them. Whether you're asked to make impromptu comments or you have a planned speech you didn't have time to prepare, getting the words right is important. The most important thing to do is to project confidence when you are unprepared. The second most important thing is to stay within your area of expertise. This will help keep your confidence high and will help you avoid saying anything foolish. In other words, silence is your best friend when you aren't prepared to answer or comment on something in a knowledgeable way.

Here are some things to say if you are unprepared to answer questions or make comments but you are spontaneously asked for your opinion.

Say This

1. "I'm not sure. I'd have to give that some thought." (Hands down, this is the best way to answer a question you don't have the answer to.)

2a. If you are pressed for your thoughts even after you express a desire to give it more thought, say: "Well, I reserve the right to edit my comments after I give this more thought, but my initial reaction is..." (Then keep it short. The fewer words, the better.)

   Or

2b. "I'd be more interested in hearing [name]'s opinion on this." (Refer to someone in your group or panel who enjoys speaking on a particular topic and has experience in it.)

Not That

1. "It's clear that..." (Avoid anything with a definite tone if you aren't absolutely sure.)

2. "Well, you know. I'm glad you asked. That is interesting..." (Avoid self-important rambling that sounds like you just want to hear your own voice. If you have something important and relevant to say, say it with as few words as possible.)

If you aren't fully prepared for something that you should have prepared for, the same principles apply. Stick with what you do know and rapidly organize the ideas. If you can present material in a list form you will be able to prepare "as you go." (This is also a great technique for when you are prepared.) For example:

Say This

1. "I'm going to cover three important things." (Even unprepared, it's relatively easy to identify how many simple points you'll cover. Keep the number under four or five so you don't get lost or confused. Three is best when unprepared. The lists are great because any time you list things, it allows your listener to recognize the beginning, middle, and end of your comments, making them easier to understand. Even more than having a visual aid, this creates the impression of a well-organized presenter.)

2. "I will keep things on this topic concise." (Assuming the topic makes sense to keep concise, this is a great way to set the stage for a shorter presentation. As a mentor of mine told me long ago, "Never say 'blah, blah, blah,' when 'blah' is enough.")

Not That

1. "I didn't have time to prepare." (This is unwise to say because many people would not ever know that if you didn't tell them. The statement is likely to reduce the perceived value of what you have to say, even if that is an unfair perception. Just leave well enough alone and do your best.)

2. "I just put some thoughts down a few minutes ago." (Even if the thoughts are great, you're

swimming upstream from the start by making the topic sound thrown together. Paradoxically, the identical thoughts could have been written two weeks earlier, and referring to the "notes you made two weeks ago" would sound impressive. Most people value forethought more than spontaneous thought.

3. "I wish I'd had more time to prepare." (Again, this makes the presentation look like it has no value.)

If you find yourself in the awkward circumstance of being completely unprepared and need more time, you are better off facing that reality head-on instead of faking something that will obviously not work. That would be an appropriate time to just say, "I am unprepared because... May I get back to you when I'm ready?" Then take your lumps and move on. In that situation, it's better to be thought less of in the short-term with a chance to redeem yourself, than to mess everything up in one unforgiving moment.

To "Take Things Back"

To be frank, there is no way of actually taking things back. Once you say them, the words are out there. But you can reduce damage with sincere and deliberate wording. Here are some ideas for when you have said too much or said damaging things.

Say This

1. "I'm sorry. I shouldn't have said that. I said it because I was upset and I lost my self-control." (Depending on the nature of the situation, you can add "and self-respect"). "It won't happen again. And I didn't mean it. My emotions got the best of me."

2. "I know I can't take that back, but I want you to know that I'm sorry."

3. (In situations that are less emotionally charged and related to misinformation). "You know what? Actually, I had that wrong. That doesn't apply here. It is completely separate. Sorry for the misstep. Let's get back on track." (The value of this statement is that it clearly separates the misinformation from the event. By stating that you "had that wrong," you discredit the information as invalid, which reduces interest in it.)

4. (If you accidentally or through weakness or gossiping share information that someone asked you to keep to yourself.) "I shouldn't have said that. It was confidential. It slipped out and I'm embarrassed by my mistake. Will you please respect that I made a mistake and keep what I just said between you and me?"

Not That

1. "Forget you heard that."

2. "Don't be so sensitive."

3. "It's just a saying [phrase, expression]."

4. "What's the big deal? I didn't mean it."

These statements are invalidating. They suggest that the other person is at fault for thinking that something wrong was said. The most important thing to do is to validate that the words you said, the ones you wish you could take back, affected them. They may have had a small effect, such as wasting a few seconds or confusing them, but they also could have hurt them emotionally.

As mentioned above, if your problem is related to gossiping, you can handle a minor mistake. If, however, this is a habit and you often tell people things about others only to regret it later, you cannot expect any words to solve your problems. I recommend giving the situation time to heal and ending the habit. This will accomplish far more than finding the right words to smooth things over.

To Ask for Something You Want

Wanting something but being nervous about asking for it is something that we all deal with. Salespeople are faced with this challenge on a daily basis and are familiar with that nervous feeling. In fact, in my experience, salespeople who lose any sense of nervousness become less effective than their counterparts who still have some nerves to manage. The same could be said about athletes or performers. Having some nerves to manage can keep you on your toes. The nerves remind you that you need to be careful to perform at your best. When you become too casual, you can lose your edge. This even happens in close personal relationships. It's good to remember that something important is at stake.

Some customer service reps, using that edge, will treat every customer, most of whom are complete strangers, with great respect. But when they come home to their loved ones, the reps lose their edge, take their families for granted, and talk in ways they never would at work. While it would be unnatural to be nervous around loved ones, the care and respect that nervousness engenders can benefit a home.

When we are nervous about asking for something, it is often because we either want to make sure our request is honored, or because we don't want to offend the person we are asking. You can use the same technique that salespeople use to manage such a situation. The key to asking for something you want is to be direct but validating. Usually the person who is responding to the request (we will call him the giver) is weighing what he loses against what he gains. The weight of what he receives must outweigh what he is giving, otherwise the transaction will not take place. Are all givers calculating or selfish? No. Nothing could be further from the truth. Sometimes people give to others without expecting anything in return. They receive the gift of virtue instead of payment. No matter what the situation, there is always something let go of and something gained.

So here is a step-by-step formula I teach salespeople and executives when they need to ask for something. I have adapted the wording to make it more universal:

1. *Make your request in as few words as possible.*
   And expect an objection.

2. *Understand and acknowledge the objection.*
   "I understand your perspective, and it makes
   sense." This is the skill of validation we've
   already discussed. It doesn't mean you agree. It
   means you understand the other party's point
   of view. Even the wording "and it makes sense"
   is about understanding another perspective. If
   other people had your understanding and your
   information, their perspective would probably
   change. Remember, this is like the example I gave
   about thinking salt is used to cool down food.
   Even mistaken beliefs can come from sensible
   ideas. Acknowledging the logic behind someone's
   beliefs doesn't mean you agree with her beliefs,
   only that her thought process makes sense to you.
   Validating people lowers the walls of defense. This
   is important because defensive people rarely give.
   (If there is no objection at all, of course, you have
   already accomplished your goal, but the likelihood
   of getting an objection is very high, even when
   you ultimately get the answer you want.)

3. *Isolate the objection and answer it.* After
   acknowledging, say "if that (the objection) were
   not the case, would you be more comfortable with
   (granting the request)?"

   a. Answering the objection means providing
      additional information that makes the giver

feel more comfortable with your request. In essence, it increases the portion of "what I get out of it." For example, if a teenager who asks to go to a party hears her dad say, "No, because you have a game tomorrow so you need your sleep," additional information might be something like the daughter saying, "But the game was cancelled." The dad gets peace of mind and a happy daughter, so he agrees to let her go out.

4. *Re-ask, based on the new information.* "So, based on that (additional information) would you (grant the request)?"

People get agitated when they are repeatedly asked the same question. If however you provide new information and re-ask the same question contingent on the new information, it lowers that risk.

Avoid these versions of responding to the objection:

Not That

1. "Is that the only reason?" (If this is said in the wrong tone, it sounds like an invalidation. If you are very good with the *way* you say things, however, this can actually be quite effective—it gets to the point.)

2. If I could change your mind on that, would you (grant the request)?" (This makes the conversation sound like a battle or challenge. It's a losing proposition because once people perceive

something to be a battle, they will often try to win for winning's sake. Don't announce that you are trying to change someone's mind. Most people like to change their own minds.)

3. "You're wrong because…" If you fail to isolate the objection, it is likely that more objections will arise, making it more difficult to re-ask each time.

While intuition plays an important role in all of our conversations, it's especially important when asking for something. Be sure to use common sense to increase your odds of success. Timing is everything.

To Self-Promote without Being Arrogant

Self -promotion can be awkward but, in some situations, it's necessary. In a job interview, you can't refuse to answer questions like "tell me about your strengths." At the same time, you don't want to sound so arrogant that you leave a bad impression. So here are some great ways to self-promote.

Say This

1. "I say this not to impress you but to impress upon you that I'm very enthusiastic about my work, and my resume highlights my enthusiasm."

(This is a great way to word this because people find enthusiasm to be genuine not arrogant.)

2. "It's awkward for me to self–promote, but I know it's necessary to share my track record. In light

of that…" (Oddly enough, if this is said with the wrong tone it can sound arrogant. Say it with a smile and with confidence. Be sincere.) Pointing out the awkwardness acknowledges to the other person that you are self-aware and not shameless in self-promotion. This can make the difference between being perceived as a prideful bragger and a confident professional.

3. "I had the privilege of working for five years with [name], which allowed me to learn [particular skill] and as a result produced [results]."

   a. This three-step statement gives you a chance to acknowledge your mentors and teachers, which subtly gives them credit as opposed to taking it yourself.

   b. It shows that you are teachable, which implies humility.

   c. By mentioning results, it presents a solid reason to believe your credentials. This is the basis of the popular saying, "If it's true, it ain't braggin'."

Not That

1. "I'm the best at…"

   In some situations, this may come off as confident, but unless you literally are the best from an objective perspective, it's risky and sounds arrogant. Try instead, "I have been trained by the best. I had access to the best. I worked my hardest to acquire this skill..."

2. "I have the answers to..."

    This may be true, but it's better to say, "I have access to the answers." Or, "I have acquired the answers." Or, "I learned the answers from..." This kind of answer conveys humility by acknowledging that you do not own the answers for yourself, even if you have relatively exclusive access to them. That role is reserved for the Newtons and Einsteins of the world.

To bolster confidence or build someone up

It's tragic when your good intentions are misunderstood. This can be especially perplexing when your words are taken in the exact opposite spirit from what you meant. The situation is worst when you are dealing with someone who is already feeling fragile, and you are trying to build them up or to bolster their confidence. The misunderstanding hurts someone who is already in a rough spot. So avoid common mistakes. Here are some well-intentioned mistakes that many make when attempting to instill confidence as well as some useful alternatives:

Not That

1. "You're almost as good at that as your [relative of any type]..."

Most people don't like to be compared to their relatives unless the observation is that they are *better* than their relative. Not everyone is sensitive to this, but you're better off not risking it at all.

2. "You've been really a pleasure to work with lately" (in reference to a rocky relationship, personal or professional).

   "Lately? What? You're saying that I am normally not?" That is the response you will get by that sort of comment. Leave out the "lately" and just say you enjoy their company.

3. "You're really good at…"

   This statement sounds like a winner but is not as effective as encouraging their efforts. If you are trying to bolster confidence, it is usually because the person is not feeling satisfied with their performance. If you just stamp it with full approval, in a way that communicates that they have already arrived and don't have any more progress to make, they will be disconnected from you.

3. "You're awesome…" (Or, "you're the man," or whatever general term not followed by a reason)

   This can be perceived as insincere. It might work the first time, but if the relationship is ongoing, eventually you'll have to give details.

4. "You're really good at that for a [girl, University of Such and Such grad, etc.]"

    a. Although this statement can be said in the spirit of teasing, it's unwise to use it unless you really know the person well. And even then it's risky.

    b. It's unwise to make these statements unless there is a clear need to reference whatever sets them apart. An example of a positive statement might be: "You're really good at that for a beginner."

Say This

1. "I'm really impressed by… "

    Then give details. The more, the better.

2. "That progress is something I would be proud of if I got that result when I was new…"

    a. Almost any reference to improvement is inspiring to most people. Notice that I suggest, "I would be proud if I got that result" instead of "you should be proud of that." This is a subtle difference, but this nuance really enhances believability. It declares that the result meets your own standard, not just a lower standard for them. Of course if you can't sincerely offer that compliment, don't—being insincere is the worst approach to take.

3. "I've really been enjoying watching you do your work. It continues to be excellent."

This is different from saying "Great job!" because this statement presumes that the work will continue to be high-level.

4. "It's exciting for me to watch this unfold. Well done so far."

(If the job is complete, then leave off "so far.")

5. "I'm becoming a big fan of your work."

This again presumes continued progress, and it is a fun thing—most of us in everyday life like to have fans.

There are many more ways to say these things, but you want to rely on the theme more than the words. By theme, I mean that the best is yet to come. If the idea is to inspire, then you want to make sure people feel a desire to continue to improve. Inspiration moves people forward. Praise alone can produce apathy and in some cases an ego that becomes difficult to work with. Inspiration, on the other hand, motivates people to improve.

To Answer Tough Questions

"Does this make me look fat?" This question has led to much unnecessary conflict, often between men and women. You could take the simple approach and just say, "No, of course not," but most women are looking for more. They want to know that they look beautiful, not just "not fat." So it's a good idea to answer with "Of course not—you look terrific," or something similar.

That simple formula can be applied to any situation where a person is asking a question that really means, "Tell me I'm acceptable to you." In the workplace, an employee might be wondering if he is meeting your standards by asking you what you think of his work. No doubt, there are times where you must tactfully express dissatisfaction in order to train him to higher standards. But keep in mind that most people perform better when they are confident. So, if possible, it's better to address the moment with something positive and then, if need be, correct him at a later time.

It is wise for you to establish expectations and standards long before the question of your approval comes up, so if that type of question is asked, then even before you answer, the asker will already have a strong sense of whether or not he is meeting the standard. Here are some good replies to similar questions:

Say This

1. "This work is excellent."

   a. Then list all the things you like about it. Tell the person in detail.

   b. After that, ask her for permission to critique her work. Although it's your job to critique it, this is still a good approach. Try: "Would you like to hear some ways that you can build upon the excellent work you're already doing?" She will reply, "Yes" in most situations. This allows you

---

to provide feedback that she sees as building on her own insight, instead of replacing her work with your ideas altogether.

2. [Answering with a question] "What do you think of it so far?"

a. If you put the question back to her, you'll see what she's thinking. If she is critical of her own work, which is common, you can build her up with the following: "Really? I think I like it even more than you. I'm glad that you have such high standards. That's something I've always liked about you. In light of your high standards, my guess is that you want constructive feedback and just saying 'good job' will not satisfy that need. So here are some thoughts on how you can take it to the next level…"

b. If she is impressed with herself, you can agree in order to validate her. If the work needs to improve, you can ask, "Are there any plans you have to improve on this?" This might take the wind out of her sails a bit, but if it is necessary to get a better result, it's a good option. She will probably tell you how she intends to take her work to the next level. In that case if you see merit in her plans, you can simply express your satisfaction with her standards again. If you find her solutions don't address the problems you see, you could suggest that she needs further training to continue to improve. Hopefully she will have had a chance to work on these issues before the subject of your approval of her work comes up again.

Part Three
MOTIVATING OTHERS TO BE THEIR BEST

❧ *Seven* ❧

"DO AS I SAY, NOT AS I DO!" WHY WORDS ARE NEVER JUST WORDS

E VERYONE KNOWS THAT leaders don't always practice what they preach. But it's a myth to suppose that a leader can only be effective if he lives perfectly according to what he teaches. Most leaders fall short but at least try to live in the spirit of what they advocate. They strive to follow their own advice, but they sometimes fall short because of their own high standards. It is, in fact, their failures that often make them aware of the importance of reinforcing behaviors. They say to themselves, "Hey, if I struggle with this, then I'm sure my team faces similar struggles."

When you *Say This, Not That,* you can jumpstart, nuance, motivate, and repair relationships. But ultimately, actions will trump words. So you'll also need to *Do This, Not That.* Unfortunately, this sometimes feels nearly impossible.

One of my first mentors, a man I found very inspiring, predicted his own demise without knowing it. He was a multimillionaire who started his own company, had tens of thousands of admirers, and a robust image. He was the kind of guy who appeared to have everything together in life. In fact, he taught the importance of balance, integrity, hard work, and everything else that fit that sort of theme.

But after he hit a rough patch with some business relationships, he changed substantially. He began acting in ways that were inconsistent with the man I knew. I can remember telling him about one of the books I was planning on writing on the subject of living in balance and having high standards in your personal and professional life.

His reaction to the project shocked me, since he was one of the people who had first inspired me to think about these things. When I asked him for feedback on the project, he said, "If you write that book, you'll need to be that person first. That is not the type of pressure I would want for myself." He slowly unraveled and become only a faint version of who I thought he was. He lost everything material, but more than that, he lost the respect of his peers and subordinates. He went from being able to influence people very easily to being disregarded when he spoke.

I suspect that one reason for his demise was that he was confused about how perfect a leader must be in order to influence others. He crumbled under the false belief that a leader must perfectly follow his own advice without fail, otherwise he forfeits the right to speak about high standards. To this day, I am not sure precisely what happened to alter his path in life, but I do know that the undue pressure he put on himself was a catalyst to his downfall.

There's no shortage of sports analogies in the work place. They are effective because they conjure up appropriate images of hard work, strategy, team effort, and last minute rallies for victory. A less common but practical analogy is that of families. This example is used less often for several reasons, including the fact that the analogy places a leader as a parent and the subordinates as children. This is an obviously offensive picture to paint for sensitive followers, which is unfortunate because the example can be very useful. The picture works because great leaders, like great parents, should try to protect their respective worlds. It is also a powerful parallel because both children and subordinates expect the highest conduct from their respective leaders.

With this analogy as the backdrop I can remember a parent once quipping to me, "Who am I to tell my kids not to be promiscuous or smoke pot? I did those things. Telling them to avoid them makes me feel like a hypocrite. It seems wrong." But it is wrong? Think of parents who smoke cigarettes or even marijuana but warn their children against these vices. In that circumstance, the kids have a strong likelihood of falling into the same practices as their parents despite the warnings because, as you know, actions speak louder than words. It is clearly the duty and obligation of parents to use their actions today to guide their children away from making mistakes, regardless of the errors of their personal past.

What happens when a leader, who is not motivated and who hides behind a big desk, asks his team to be motivated? Is this wrong and unethical or just not effective? While she certainly is leading ineffectively,

I'd argue that the lazy leader has the same obligation to motivate her team as the motivated leader, despite her own personal struggles. Leaders are often part of the problems that organizations face. The growing process may involve leaders raising their own standards. It may not be practical or possible for a leader to "master" herself prior to asking her team to do the same.

I'm not sure what emotions or thoughts this concept triggers in you personally, but I have worked with many leaders who struggle with this sort of challenge. Some leaders find themselves privately muddling their own daily responsibilities which causes them to take a similar position to a parent who acts laissez faire. They basically say to themselves, "How can I ask my team to be motivated when I am not motivated myself?" In a twisted way, both the parent and the leader are motivated by a fear of hypocrisy. For "ethical" reasons they want to avoid being hypocritical so they become permissive leaders.

The easy advice here is to tell both the leader and the parent to get their acts together and to preach the corresponding behaviors to their followers. In other words, to tell them, "Say this not that, and do this not that." But it is difficult to practice what you preach at times. So, in the meantime, leaders must preach what is good no matter what.

A second analogy makes this point clear. You want your doctor to give you good advice regardless of what she practices in her own life. If she tells you to cut out saturated fat and to quit smoking because it causes heart disease, it does not matter whether or not her next act is to order a cheeseburger at a fast food joint or to smoke a cigarette. Her obligation is to advise you appropriately regardless of her personal practices.

As a leader, you will be challenged by your own moral struggles and shortcomings, but all along the way you must encourage the people you lead to be their best and to pursue the highest standards. We all struggle. The only true hypocrite is the person who stops trying to improve or who claims perfection for himself. Being assigned a position of leadership does not mean that you have arrived at perfection. It is more likely that you demonstrate the character to improve or to recommit after you fall short. Give your team the gift of full conviction to high standards regardless of your past or current struggles and then work towards them on your own. Do your best to *Say This, Not That* and to *Do This, Not That*.

ENDNOTES

1   Her purpose was to determine the importance of being
     personally connected to one another via technology.
     She had researched the connection that people
     have both face to face and via instant messaging.
     She defines connection as "multidimensional space
     comprised of feelings of affinity, commitment, and
     attention." The report goes on to say that, "These
     dimensions of connection must be kept in a state
     of sufficient excitation or activation to promote
     effective communication in which participants
     can exchange information." In ethnographic
     investigations of instant messaging in the workplace
     (Nardi et al., 2000) and communication in personal
     social networks in the workplace (Nardi et al., 2002;
     Nardi and Whittaker, 2002), open-ended interviews
     yielded many data that seemed to have little to do
     with the kinds of communicative activity suggested
     by the need for information bandwidth. The data
     pointed instead to activity geared to establishing
     feelings of connection with others for the purpose
     of continued interactions over time. A feeling of
     connection is a subjective state in which a person
     experiences an openness to interacting with another
     person. The ethnographic data showed that feelings of
     connection were accomplished through interactions
     involving (1) the body and (2) informal discourse

of low information content. This paper distinguishes between communicative activity that establishes feelings of connection that ready people for further interaction with each other, and communicative activity in which information is exchanged. It is proposed that activities of connection establish a field of connection between dyads in which social and affective connections are stimulated in order to ready people for further communication (typically of an informational nature). A field of connection is a labile multidimensional space comprised of feelings of affinity, commitment, and attention. These dimensions of connection must be kept in a state of sufficient excitation or activation to promote effective communication in which participants can exchange information. The paper describes the work of creating and sustaining connection as it emerged in informants' accounts. An argument is made that such work is central to communication and has not been a focus of previous research on computer-mediated communication.

Crossroad Books for
Your Leadership Library

For leaders of all kinds, Crossroad offers books to help you move to a deeper level. Here is just a few of our books you should know about.

If you have ever wondered if there is a better way to decide how to spend your money and whom to donate to, this next book is essential reading. In *What Your Money Means: And How to Use It Well,* Frank J. Hanna challenges us to think about our money in a different way. If we are honest, even in these difficult financial times many of us have more than we need for mere survival. The chapters of this book lead us to identify what our essential needs are and how best to use the money that is not essential.

If you have had enough experience as the leader of a group to witness both the successes and downturns of an organization, you will benefit from *The Soul of a Leader: Finding Your Path to Success and Fulfillment.* Drawing from real-life stories, Margaret Benefiel identifies several of the key challenges that organizations face in times of transition. She suggests practical, specific steps for identifying and strengthening the mission statement, putting it in place, and most importantly, remaining creative and flexible when setbacks occurs.

Staying true to your mission is also the central theme in Dave Durand's *Win the World Without Losing Your Soul.* This book takes on the idea that high levels of success can only come at the cost of personal integrity. Drawing from his own work consulting with organizations and seeing what works and doesn't work, Durand strengthens our ability to remain true to our convictions and true to our ambitions for success.

ABOUT THE AUTHOR

OVER 100,000 PEOPLE from all walks of life—sales representatives, Fortune 500 CEOs, secretaries, educators, small business owners, and even stay-at-home parents – have learned from Dave Durand's training. In his speeches, individual coaching, CDs, and books, he offers people tested, easy to understand, practical solutions for transforming their professional and personal lives.

Dave began his career as a college student selling Cutco Cutlery, demonstrating his success by becoming the youngest person in the company's 55-year history to be inducted into the company's Hall of Fame. He would later oversee the Canadian operation and a 15-state region in the U.S. While continuing his success at Vector, in 1998, Dave founded ProBalance, Inc.™, a time management efficiency and leadership effectiveness company that helps individuals, corporations, and associations maximize the use of their time and develop leaders to their fullest potential.

Dave first put his ideas into book form with *Perpetual Motivation: How to Keep Your Fire Burning in Your Career and in Life*. This memorable discussion of how to find balance in life and work became a national bestseller, ranked #1 on Amazon for three months in its field. He followed this with *Win the World without Losing Your Soul*.

For more information on Dave's work, or to invite Dave as a speaker to your organization, please visit DaveDurand.com.